# How to Become a Freelance Writer and Get Paid Now

## A Step-by-Step Guide to

## Your First Paycheck in a Week or Less

### By

### Shyley MacFarland

## Copyright Notice

CreateSpace Independent Publishing Platform

Copyright © 2012 by Shyley MacFarland
First Printing, 2012

ISBN-13:
978-1478373452

ISBN-10:
1478373458

## *<u>Disclaimer</u>*

# Table of Contents

# *Part 1: General Information to Get You Started*

This book is divided into three parts, and each part has sections and sub-sections as well. This will make it easier for you to get to the information that you need. The first part - this part - covers general information that you need to get started, and although you are probably in a hurry to get right to the meat of the matter, you should not skip this section, because it could mean the difference between success and failure as a freelance writer.

In this section, we will cover:

- What this Guide Is and What It Is Not
- The Tools You Need to Get Started
- The Skills You Need as a Freelance Writer
- How to Keep Track of Everything and Why You Should Do So
- The Importance and Value of Starting Small and Growing
- The Importance of Scheduling Your Work Time
- Where and Why to Start a Blog Immediately

Let's get the ball rolling so you can start making money as a freelance writer and get paid within a week.

## - Introduction -
### What this Guide Is and What It Is Not

Do you dream of writing for a living? Do you dream of quitting your job, setting your own hours, and having more freedom and money to do the things that you want in life? Do you dream of seeing your work and your name in print? Do you dream of fame and fortune, and possibly even a Pulitzer Prize? Do you want to be the next Danielle Steele or the next Mark Twain?

We all have those dreams. Now, let's get back to reality.

Today, you most likely dream of having an extra income, or having enough money to pay your bills. That is what this guide is. Here, you will learn how to do this very quickly. This guide will teach you how to become a part time or fulltime freelance writer, and how to make the income that you need to pay your bills, in a very realistic manner.

This guide does not teach you how to write. It is assumed that you already know how to write, and that you do it reasonably well. With that said, later we will touch on the skills that you need as a freelance writer, and where to get help if you need to hone those skills.

This guide does not teach you how to price your freelancing skills, or how to query magazines and publishers. Writing for magazines, writing books and things of this nature are what your ultimate goal as a freelance writer should be and you should definitely be working towards that - but in the meantime, you need an income.

This guide will show you which freelancing websites to use, and how to use them effectively to begin earning money immediately. Established freelance writers - those who are already being published in books, magazines, and other outlets - are largely against the use of these websites because of the low pay involved.

That's right - low pay, but enough pay to support you and pay your bills while you work towards becoming a higher level freelance writer. Too often, those who want to be freelance writers fail simply because they allow their pride and self worth to get between them and success.

In any type of job, you have to start at the bottom and work your way up the proverbial food chain - and freelance writing is no different. So, while you are making a living by being a working freelance writer, those other people who are trying to establish themselves as freelance writers are turning their noses up in the air and saying "I would never work for such low rates." Well, they don't have to work for these low rates. The can continue to dream, and continue to work at that 9- 5 job that has nothing to do with writing, and they can continue to fail as freelance writers, keeping their pride intact the whole while. This just means that you have less competition for the moment.

This isn't about pride and self worth at all. It is not about the ongoing debate between writers and publishers about what is and is not fair in terms of rates. It's about breaking into this exclusive freelancing world and being successful at it right from the get-go, and getting an income that will allow you to go after those bigger dreams that you have.

To recap, this guide will:

- Teach you how and where to start earning money right now.
- Teach you how to reach your immediate income needs.
- Point you in the right direction if you need to hone up on your writing skills.

This guide will not:

- Teach you how to write.
- Teach you how to query magazine editors or publishers.
- Teach you how to write a book and get published.
- Teach you how to find private clients.
- Teach you how to set rates for your writing skills.

# *Tools You Need to Get Started as a Freelance Writer*

As with any other type of profession, there are certain tools that are required in order to start your freelance writing career. Fortunately, these tools will not cost you anything at all, and they are very simple to obtain.

You need:

- Word Processing Software
- A computer with an internet connection
- A way to collect your payments

I will assume that you already have a computer with an internet connection, but if you do not, you need to know that this is definitely a requirement if you plan to use the information in this book to get your freelance writing career started. It does not matter which type of computer you have, and in the grand scheme of things, it doesn't matter how fast or slow your internet connection is - although you will work more efficiently and earn money faster with a faster connection and a decent computer.

In terms of word processing software, there are many options. The key thing is that you need to be able to put your writing in .doc format. This requires either Microsoft Word, which can be expensive if you do not already have it, or Open Office, which is the free alternative to Microsoft Office, and can be downloaded from www.openoffice.org. You can also create documents using Google Docs, but you will be better off in the long run to use Microsoft Word or Open Office.

For payments, you need a PayPal account. You can open a free PayPal account at www.paypal.com. The account type that is most recommended is a Premium Account. Most freelance websites pay via PayPal, so it is essential to have an account. You also need to go ahead and get the PayPal debit card that is attached to your account as well. This debit card is also free, and this will allow you to withdraw your PayPal funds directly from an ATM instead of having to transfer funds to a bank account.

Here is the checklist once more:

- You need a computer.

- You need an internet connection.

- You need word processing software (Microsoft Word or Open Office).

- You need a free Premium PayPal account from www.paypal.com.

# Skills You Need as a Freelance Writer

The ability to type does not make you a writer. I cannot stress this enough. In order to be a successful freelance writer, you need to be able to produce content that is not only engaging and factual, but also free of grammar and spelling mistakes. You need to be able to string sentences together so that the information flows in a logical, easy to read manner.

Not everyone has those skills naturally. Unfortunately, many people also think that their writing is 'good enough' when it is actually atrocious. Poor writing skills can ruin your reputation as a freelance writer before you even get started, and that is why it is essential that you take this next recommendation very seriously.

### Test your writing skills before you do anything else.

This can be done for free at www.edufind.com/english/grammar/. The test takes twenty minutes, and you can find out what level your writing skill is at. You do not want to start writing through any freelance sites without first taking this test to ensure that your writing skills are up to par.

If your writing skills are not up to par, this does not mean that you cannot be a freelance writer. It just means that it's not going to happen for you today. There are countless free writing courses available online, as well as grammar courses and English courses. Find one and start honing your English, grammar, and writing skills right away. I highly recommend the free course offered through About University at esl.about.com/c/ec/20.htm.

Not all writers have perfect grammar and spelling. Fortunately, Microsoft Word and Open Office have built in spell checkers and grammar checkers. However, there are a couple of websites that freelance writers find highly useful when they are not sure about the grammar that they have used. You can check your grammar at www.grammarly.com.

Although this doesn't really fall under the heading of 'skills,' you do need to know what will be expected of you when working through these freelance sites. Many people cannot succeed through these sites because they get hung up on small details. Additionally, they go into it not fully understanding what the clients or buyers on these sites are looking for.

For the most part, these buyers - the people who will hire you to do these writing jobs - are not looking for a thesis or dissertation. They are not looking for 6000 word essays. Instead, they are looking for content that they can use on their websites, blogs, or that they can submit to article directories. Most of the writing that you will be doing is ghostwriting. This means that the client is paying you for the work, and he or she owns the copyright to that work as soon as it is paid for. Additionally, he or she has the right to take your name off of the writing, change the writing, and do whatever he or she wants with the writing.

The writing that you will generally be articles that are between 150 and 1000 words. It is rare to have a request for articles that are shorter or longer than that, and the average length of articles requested are actually between 400 words and 600 words. As you can imagine, it is very difficult to cover any topic in depth in such few words. That is not the goal of your client, however. Normally, his goal is to provide content on his website or blog that is keyword optimized to draw the attention of the search engines, and written well enough to give his website visitors valuable information at the same time.

So, how can you really know whether your writing will cut it in this type of setting? Take a look at what is generally expected and learn from it. Visit www.ezinearticles.com and start reading articles. Pay attention to how short those articles are and how they are structured. Many clients that you will write for will be submitting the work to this website for promotional reasons, so this is the best place to figure out what most of your clients will expect from you.

Here is another checklist for you to follow:

   - Take the writing test at www.edufind.com/english/grammar/.

   - Find a free writing course or use the one at esl.about.com/c/ec/20.htm.

   - Familiarize yourself with Grammarly at www.grammarly.com.

   - Study the format of articles at www.ezinearticles.com

## *Keeping Track of Everything*

The quickest way to fail is to not try at all. The second quickest way to fail is to be disorganized. You need to keep track of everything right from the start. At the same time, you do not want to spend all of your time getting organized. Do not get lost in the details.

Here is what you need to keep track of:

- Website addresses where you find work.

- Your username and passwords for those sites.

- Your income for tax purposes.

- Your expenses (if you have any) for tax purposes.

- Article topics that sell well.

Again, you do not want to spend a lot of time on this. For now, just open up a Word document or use notepad, or a pen and a piece of paper to jot down this information. You can arrange it into powerful programs or whatever you want to do later on. Remember that your goal in this is to start earning money, not to just plan to earn money.

I personally use OneNote, which is a by product of Microsoft Office. I love it because I can set up folders, sections, pages, subpages and so forth, and this allows me to keep all of the information that I need inside one program. It took me a while to get it arranged 'just so' but in the end that time was well spent. Of course, I set this up on one of my non-writing days, when I wasn't working to earn the money that I wanted, and I suggest that you set your record keeping system up on one of your non-writing days as well.

I also keep my bookmarks in my web browser well organized. This saves me lots of time when writing articles. I am constantly finding that I write about the same topics over and over again. So, when I do quick research for a topic that I am not knowledgeable about, I bookmark resources. I then organize those bookmarks into folders, and label those folders by topic. I save lots of time because I do not have to search over and over again for the same or similar information when writing articles.

Again, keep track of everything, but do not allow this to suck your time away right now.

## *Start Small and Grow*

When you start out as a freelance writer, it is essential that you start small, and then grow once you know what your capabilities are in terms of time. It is very easy to get very overloaded, in a very short period of time - especially when you write well, and buyers start realizing that.

When I first started out as a freelancer in 2001, I needed money, and I needed it fast. Unfortunately, back then, freelancing sites were few and far between, and there was a great deal of competition. I quickly learned how to underbid everyone - because of my need for money - but I was also bidding on every job that I could find that I felt qualified to do.

One time, I bid on twenty different jobs. Imagine my surprise when I woke up the next morning, logged into the site, and found that I had won all of those jobs. I was excited, until I started looking at deadlines, and wondering just how many articles I could do in a day. I had a solid week of working almost non-stop, getting very little sleep, in order to meet those deadlines.

I can tell you from experience that you shouldn't go about getting work in that way. I advise you to start small, and add work as you feel you can handle it. Fortunately, the first site that you will work through does not require bidding at all. Instead, you simply find an article that you are interested in writing, click the button, and immediately write the article. You then submit the article, the buyer either approves it or rejects it, and if it is approved, the money is added to your account.

While many freelance writers turn their noses into the air and sniff at such a site, I actually enjoy working through that site to this very day. That site allows me to control my income fairly well, while working on my own schedule. It isn't possible to overload yourself with that site, which I will be covering in great detail later on.

It is the sites where you bid for jobs that it is easy to get overloaded on. One day, you might not win any bids, and the next day, you may win them all. This is why I advise you to start small and grow. To follow the plan laid out in this book, your weekly income will be derived from the site I talked about previously - where you control the deadline, so to speak, by selecting and writing one article at a time.

The next site that you will work through is a bid site, and the third type of website that you will work through is a paid for content site. You will do work through each site each day in most cases, but for the bid sites, I suggest that you only bid on one or two jobs at a time, until you know how much work you are capable of finishing each day.

With the bid sites, it is harder to control your income, because you do not know if or when you will win jobs. The buyers have a certain amount of time to choose a winning bidder, but they also reserve the right to not choose a bidder at all, causing a cancellation of the bid request.

So, why should you even consider working through the bid sites if you can earn money at will through the other site? In all honesty, it is because you will earn more money per job through the bid sites, so you do want to start building your reputation through those sites, but understand that you will have a harder time controlling your overall income.

The paid for content sites are also not sites where you have control over your income. Instead, these sites should be viewed as sites that will bring you income over time, as opposed to bringing you income this week. All three types of sites have a role in our plan to earn a living as a freelance writer, so you want to use all three methods simultaneously, but not overload yourself in the process.

Another site, which can be quite profitable, is a site where I write content on topics of my choice, and buyers can purchase the articles that I have written. These articles sell for top dollar, and this is something else I will cover in great detail. But, this is also another site where I really cannot control my overall income - it is just a matter of what buyers come along to purchase content, what topics they are looking for, and whether or not I have content on those topics in my inventory.

Here is my personal formula for the success that I have achieved in my freelance writing career:

Each day that I work, I work in this exact order:

   - I bid on one job at my favorite bid site, unless I have a job already in progress through that site. If I already have a job in progress, I do x number of articles for that job based on my deadline, making sure that I've allowed myself time to write through the site where I have greater control of my income.

   - I do x number of jobs through the non-bid site, based on how much money I want or need to earn that day.

   - I write one article for the paid content site that I like best.

   - I write and submit one article to the site where my content is sold.

   - I update my blogs. I have two blogs that I add posts to each day.

   - I write for me. This book is an example of 'writing for me.' It essentially means that I am writing for income, but not for a client or buyer.

As you can see, there are six parts to my work day, and how much time I spend on each activity is very important, because this affects my income. Let's take a closer look at the six parts of my day.

1. Bid site: I always make sure that I have one job in progress through this site. I usually go for jobs that are short, meaning that they are jobs to just do five or ten articles. I have been working through this site for years, and I have a stellar reputation. Retaining that reputation is vital to me. At the same time, I don't really rely on this site for my income, because my income would then be too unpredictable and varied.

Total Time Spent for this Site: Between 15 minutes and 2 hours, depending on the scope of the job in progress.

2. Non Bid Site: I have Elite status on this site, so I am able to take the jobs that pay the highest. I know how much money I want or need to earn each day. I usually do ten articles each day on this site to reach my daily income goal of $100. It is important to note here that I type 96 words per minute with 100% accuracy, and I've been doing this for a long time, so it doesn't take me more than 15 minutes to write a 500 word article, but for more complex articles, it can take up to 30 minutes.

Total Time Spent for this Site: Anywhere from 2.5 hours to 5 hours.

3. Paid Publishing Site: I write one article per day for this site.

Total Time Spent for this Site: 30 minutes.

4. Sell Content Site: I write one article per day for this site. This takes me approximately fifteen or twenty minutes.

Total Time Spent for this Site: 30 minutes.

5. Update Blogs: One post for each blog each day.

Total Time Spent: 30 minutes

6. Write for Me: The time spent on this activity is varied, and depends on how much time I have left in my work day, but I do make it a point to spend at least one hour on this activity each day.

Total Time Spent: 1 Hour

My total time spent for all of this work is between five and nine hours per day, and as you can see, the activity that gets the majority of the time is the one that allows me to control my income the most.

It is also important to note that on some days, I do not work through the non bid site at all. The only time that I skip this site is when I have a job in progress through the bid site that replaces that income to my satisfaction. With that said, however, the non-bid site pays me each week, whereas the bid site only pays me three times per month.

The site where my content is sold is completely unpredictable. I may make several sales during a week - or absolutely no sales. If I wake up one day and see that I have made $100 or more in sales through that site, I can skip the non-bid site, and spend time on my own writing work, or choose to go ahead and work through the non-bid site to earn additional income for that week.

Money that I make from my blogs and from books is completely unpredictable. I do derive income from those activities, but it is too varied to count on when it comes to making the money that I need to pay my bills, and advertising revenue from those sites is only paid out monthly, as are royalties from books.

That is my day. Since you are just starting out, that most likely will not be your day. Your day will mostly be writing through the non-bid site, while growing your freelance business as you see fit. Add slowly to your business, only taking on what you are comfortable with, and only adding one element at a time.

You may wonder why I work through so many different channels, and that is a good question to ask. Life is unpredictable, and so is the Internet. My favorite non-bid site could be here today and gone tomorrow, as could my favorite bid site. I could go a week or two without getting any income at all through any of the unpredictable income channels, or through the site where my content is sold. By using different channels of income, I secure myself financially, regardless of what life or the Internet brings.

With that said, even if I cannot write each day, I know that I will eventually derive income through the paid publishing platforms, through book sales, and through advertising revenue on my blogs. Regardless of how unpredictable that income is, there is income. It is largely about ensuring that I have income coming from multiple sources, as well as generating passive income. In case you are not familiar with the term, passive income is essentially income that is derived from doing something once and getting revenue or income from it repeatedly over time. The royalties from this book is an example of passive income, and that is what I am personally shooting for - more passive income, which allows me to write when I want to write, on topics that I choose to write about.

## *Schedule Your Work Time*

You may think we have covered this, but we haven't. Knowing how many hours you need to work each day is one thing. Scheduling that time is something altogether different. Freelance writing isn't like going to a regular 9 to 5 job. Regardless of what type of writing you are doing, or who you are doing that writing for, writing is a creative process, and you need to schedule your work time for the time of the day when you are most creative.

Most people will tell you to schedule your work time when you will have the fewest interruptions. Do not listen to that advice. Schedule your work time for when you are most creative, and then make sure that the time you've decided upon will be uninterrupted.

Here are some tips:

- Make sure your friends and family know when your work time is, and ask them not to interrupt you during this time.

- Try to work out of everyone else's path. The kitchen table is not ideal. A home office is perfect, especially if it has a door that you can close and lock. If you don't have a home office, move your computer into your bedroom. You need a quiet place to work, where your thought processes will not be interrupted.

- Turn off the ringer on your home phone and cell phone, and let all calls go to voicemail. Put your cell phone out of reach, or better yet, out of the room where you are working.

- Turn off the television.

- Do not check your email, Facebook, or anything else on your computer while you are writing.

Working as a freelancer takes real self control. It is so easy to allow distractions to keep you from accomplishing what you need to accomplish. If you want to earn the income that you need, and you want to succeed as a freelancer, you absolutely must practice self control. Make it a habit to work during your scheduled work time right from the beginning. Checking your Facebook page is not work related, and your email does not need to be checked every five minutes.

My most creative time is at night. I work all night, and I sleep during the day. I do this for a few reasons:

1. This is the time that I am most creative. I've been a night owl my entire life. This is when my mind works best, my thoughts are very clear, and I feel my most energetic.

2. I don't have any interruptions because everyone I know is asleep...except for one other person.

3. That other person is my husband, who happens to work nights, so my nighttime creativity works out well for us.

When I come into my home office, I turn on my computer, check my email, check my Facebook page, close those pages in my browser, and get to work. I will not open my email or Facebook again until my work for the day is complete.

I have scheduled breaks throughout the night, and my husband is aware of when those breaks are. He calls me on those breaks, and only on those breaks. I could use those breaks to check email, surf the web, or check Facebook should I want to do that, but I don't. I check those things twice each day - right before I start work, and right after I am finished for the day.

You must do what works for you, in terms of scheduling your work, but make sure that you schedule the work first, and then schedule everything else around that. Because this type of work does require creativity, it really cannot work in any other way successfully.

As you progress in your freelance writing career, refer to the previous chapter in this book, and work your various income producing activities into the time that you have set aside for writing as you see fit, based on your income goals. As you continue to grow as a freelance writer, you will know how much time you need to spend on each activity, so this will be easy to schedule.

Make sure that you don't burn yourself out. One of the biggest mistakes that many freelance writers make is working every waking hour. If you follow the methods in this book, you can have a successful career as a freelance writer, making the income that you want to make, and have a life aside from your career as well. Schedule work time, but make sure that you are scheduling off work time as well. I make it a point to never work on weekends. I use the creative time on weekends to enjoy other creative things that do not involve writing, such as needlework, sketching, gardening, cooking, and things of this nature.

## *Start Blogging: Where and Why*

As mentioned earlier, I have two blogs that I post to each day. You need a blog as well, for several reasons. You may see this as a pointless activity, since earning money with a blog takes a great deal of time, but earning money is not the main reason that you need a blog.

When you work through the freelance sites where you have to bid on work, many buyers will ask to see samples of your work. If you have a blog, you have samples of your work readily available. You can also use your blog to link to your content on the paid publishing platforms, which improves search engine ranking for that content, and for your blog.

You can set up advertising on your blog, such as Google AdSense, and eventually earn an extra bit of money from this. Your blog can even be used to find private clients to write for. Working for private clients usually pays quite well, but you need to be established to find this type of work.

Additionally, when you work through the site where you can sell your content, you can use a widget on your blog that tells your visitors what articles you have for sale there. Trust me when I tell you that a blog is a very useful tool in the freelance writing world. You can also link to your profiles at the freelancing sites on your blog, and vice versa.

Your blog should be focused on your writing, or writing in general. So, why do I have two blogs? One of my blogs is writing related, and is called A Content Writer's Life, at www.contentwriterslife.com. The other blog is related to Lupus, at www.thelupuswayoflife.com. I have the Lupus blog because I have Lupus, and this is a topic that is very important to me personally. If you have a topic that is very important to you that has nothing to do with writing, by all means, blog about it - but on a separate blog from your writing related blog.

You can start a blog for free at www.blogger.com or at www.wordpress.com. Most people will tell you that you need your own domain name instead of using one of the free blogging platforms, and it is true that this is the better option. However, for now, just get started with one of the free blogs so you can get to work making money. You can always purchase a domain name and hosting later on, and export your blog to your own domain.

You do not have to post to your blog each and everyday, but you should make it a point to post to it at least once a week. If possible, post to it at least three times per week. Don't worry about getting visitors to your blog too much right now. The more you post, the more Google will love you, and the traffic will eventually build itself.

Now, there are many Internet Marketing Gurus who would like to shoot me in the head right now for giving you such advice as that, but you are in a hurry to get started as a freelance writer. You do not have time right now to build a killer, niche blog and drive traffic to it.

I'm not saying that you won't ever want to increase traffic to your blog - you will. But for now, your focus needs to be on building your freelance writing career in the most logical way possible, in the shortest amount of time possible, in order to start earning the income that you need right away. Your blog is just a tool in that endeavor at this point in time - a place to showcase your writing skills, and to link to content that you have in other places that will bring you an income faster than your blog ever could.

**This is very important:** Never post articles that you have written for clients or buyers on your blog. The work that you will be doing following the methods in this book is mostly work-for-hire work, or ghostwriting. Once you are paid for the work, it is no longer yours to use. You should also never post the names of your clients on your blog. They do not want anyone to know that they are using ghostwriters for their content.

Also remember that you will be directing potential buyers or clients to your blog to see samples of your writing skills. Do not post anything to your blog that you wouldn't want them to see.

# *Part 2: Start Writing and Get Paid*

Now, you are getting to the meat of the matter - writing and getting paid for it. In Part 2: Start Writing and Get Paid, we will cover:

- Working through Freelance Websites - Bid and No Bid Platforms

- Writing and Selling Your Content on Consignment

- Working through Paid Publishing Platforms

Throughout these pages, I will be covering the four websites that I use each day to earn a fulltime income by freelance writing in fairly extensive detail. Note that there are many more sites like these, but I do not cover those sites in detail because I do not use them.

I don't use those other sites simply because I am happy with the ones that I do use - and I cannot say that there is any reason that you should avoid those sites. For your convenience and information, I am including lists of those other sites in Part 4 of this book.

The four sites that are covered in detail in Part 2 include:

- iWriter, at www.iwriter.com

- vWorker at www.vworker.com

- Constant-Content at www.constant-content.com

- Yahoo! Contributor Network at contributor.yahoo.com

As I have mentioned, I also operate two blogs and derive royalties from books that I write. However, because income from those sources is so sporadic and unpredictable, I only count income from these four sites for the income that I depend on each week or month. I also do not cover earning money from blogging or from book sales here because those activities are beyond the scope of this book.

Are you ready to become a freelance writer and get paid? Let's get down to business!

## *Working through Freelance Websites: Bid and No Bid Platforms*

Before we dive right in, let's go over a few essential things that you need to know about freelance websites.

1. There is a lot of competition. Bring your A Game. This means that you need to write well, have decent spelling and grammar skills, and be prepared to work.

2. When you sign up for these sites, read everything that there is to read. Read the FAQ section of each site. Read the terms and conditions for each site - including the fine print. Watch any tutorial videos that are available. I realize that you are in a hurry to get started, but sometimes this information is the difference between success with a site and utter failure.

3. You can use a pen name on these sites, or your real name. It is up to you whether you use a pen name or not, but you will need to provide the freelance company with your real information - including your real name - in order to get paid. When you sign up, use the email address that is connected to your PayPal account. It is also a good idea to use the same name consistently, from one freelance site to another.

4. Fill out your profile on these sites completely. Remember that you are trying to sell your services - especially on the bidding platform sites. Make sure that you upload a picture of yourself as well. Studies have shown that those writers who include pictures in their profile win more jobs.

5. When entering bio information on your profiles, keep it professional. You want to talk about your experience as a writer. Nobody cares about your cat or how you spend your free time.

6. Most of these sites will not allow you to link to outside websites, but when you post bids, you can usually send a potential client to your blog by not formatting it as a URL. For example, instead of www.yourblog.com, you might type blog dot com. The buyer will understand what you are doing, and type the correct URL into his or her web browser.

7. Don't get all crazy and freak out about privacy concerns when you are asked for your social security number. Nobody is trying to steal your identity. This information is required because you are about to earn money. These freelance companies will be reporting your income to the IRS, and they will be sending you a 1099 form each year for your taxes. Your social security number is required.

*iWriter*
*www.iwriter.com*

At iWriter, you will start as a Standard Writer, and work your way up to Elite Status. This means that you will start working for bottom dollar. Do not be put off by this, as so many other freelancers are. It really is not that hard to reach Elite status, where you will earn anywhere from $8 to $16 or more for each article that you write.

In order to reach Elite Status, you must complete 30 assignments and have a high enough star rating. If you put your mind to it, and you really work at it, you can essentially make Elite Status in about a week. I did it by writing five articles per day, for six straight days. The trick to reaching Elite Status quickly is to only write the 150 word and 300 word articles. Yes, the pay is absolutely horrendous, but in the end, it is worth it to work for this tiny amount of money in the beginning.

At iWriter, you can choose to get paid every week or every two weeks. There is a payment threshhold of $20. That means that you won't actually receive any pay until you've earned that amount of money. Don't worry; you can earn that amount in less than a day of work, even at the lowest of rates. The funds are paid into your PayPal account on Tuesdays if you choose the weekly option. The weekly option is the one that I recommend. It feels good to get paid fast. You get paid for the work that has been approved by the buyers regardless of your status or your star rating.

Once you have signed up, make sure that you watch the tutorial for writers. This is very important. Once you've watched that video, you are ready to get to work.

*Important Note:* Do not write your articles in your own word processing software and then copy and paste it into the text box at iWriter. This causes all sorts of formatting problems.

At the same time, never submit an article without first copying it from the text box at iWriter and pasting it into your own word processing software. The word processor on the site does not check your spelling and grammar, but your own word processing software does. Find any mistakes that you have made using your own word processing software, and then switch back over to iWriter to make any needed corrections.

Once you are signed up, and you log in, you will see your dashboard. This page has lots of information on it, and you will be viewing this page often as you work. Here, you can see the top section of my own dashboard at iWriter.

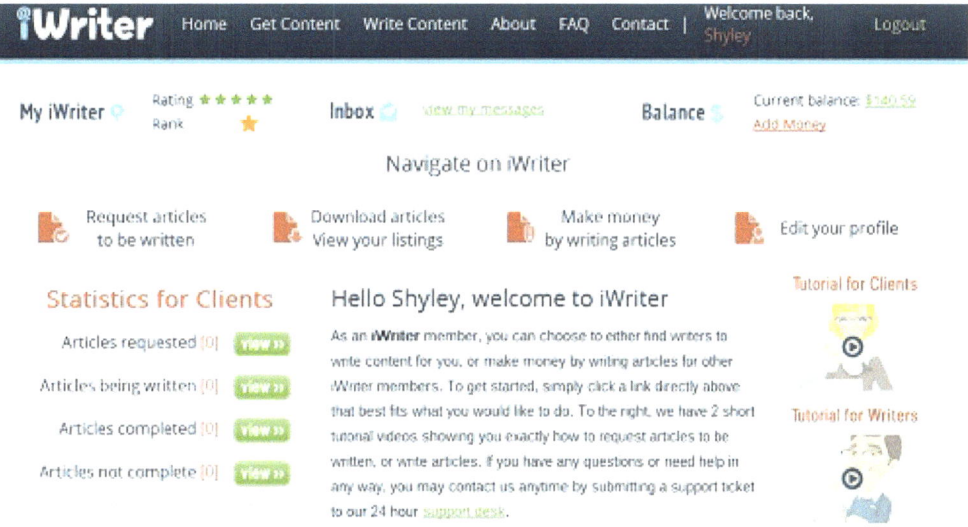

Here, you can see my star rating and rank on the upper left side of the screen. To see what your actual numbers are, just hold your mouse over the stars. From this screen you can also access your inbox to view any messages, and see your balance. This is the amount that has not yet been paid out to you, but is ready to be paid out to you on the next payday.

Here, you can see that I am owed $140.59. That, my friends, is just for one day of work on this site. The statistics screen is for clients only, and does not pertain to you. Below that is a statistics screen for writers, where you can see whether or not you have special requests, how many articles you have written, and so forth. To edit your profile, you will click on your name on the upper right hand side of the screen.

The next screen of importance to you as a writer is reached by clicking "Write Content" at the top of the dashboard page. This is where you will find the work. At the top of the page, you can still get back to your dashboard by clicking on "Home." You can still see your rating and rank, your inbox, and the money owed to you. Below that is the area where you can select options to find work that you want to do.

You can refine your search however you like, but I personally only search by word count required. The options are 150, 300, 500, 700, and 1000. As someone who is trying to reach Elite Status, stick with the 150 and 300 word requests. These short articles will get you to Elite Status quickly.

As you look through the listings for article requests on this page, you should be looking first at the requester. A requester is essentially the client or buyer at iWriter. The two things about the requester that are most important to you are:

1. His approval rating.
2. His star rating.

You can see both of these things in the second listing of this screen shot. The first listing does not have a star rating because that requester has yet to get any ratings. You want to avoid requester #1...let someone else be the guinea pig on that one. You also want to avoid requester #2 because he only has an approval rating of 38%. This means that he rejects the majority of the articles that are submitted to him. In this case, his five star rating means very little because of his approval/rejection rating.

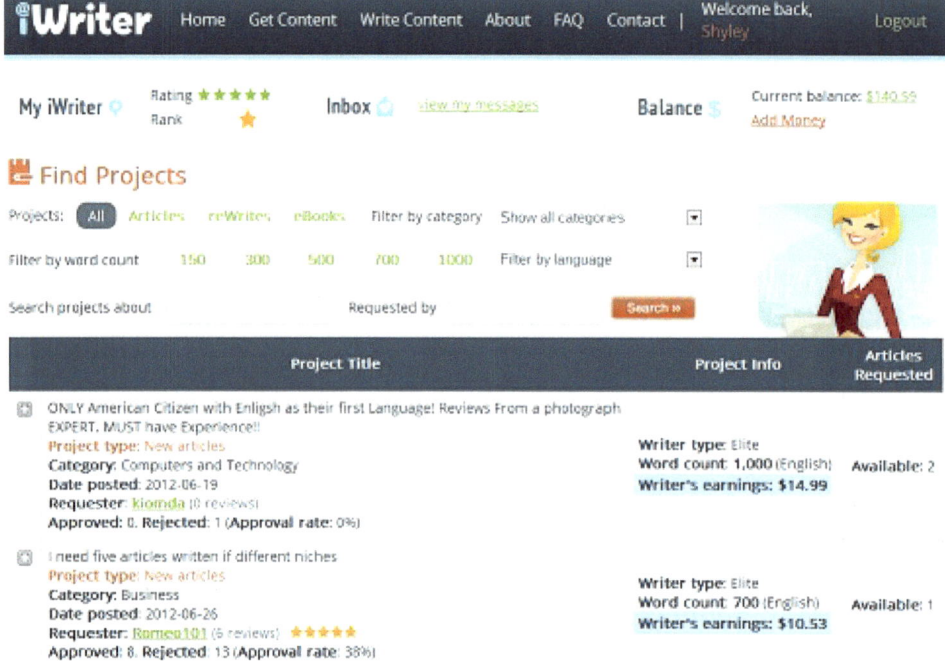

The requesters that you do want to write for should have an approval rate of at least 70%, and a star rating between four and five.

Scrolling down this page, I find a winner:

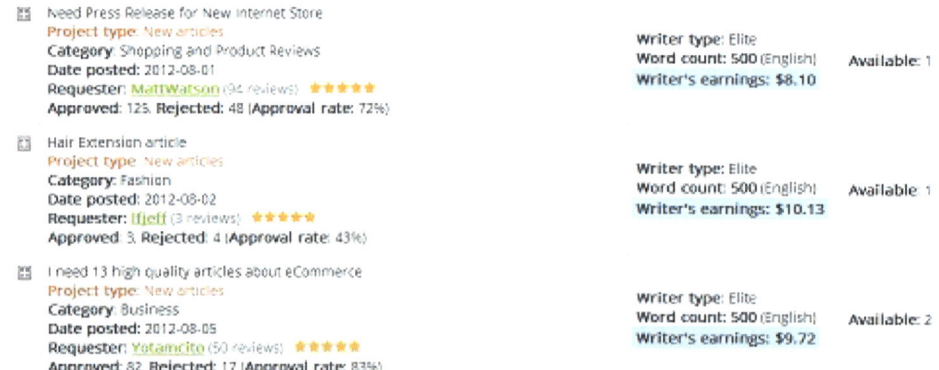

The third requester here has an approval rating of 83% and a five star rating. He wants a 500 word article, and I will be paid $9.72 for producing what he wants.

He has two jobs available. I need to click the plus sign on the left side of his listing to get more information, and this is what I see:

Here, I can see the keywords that he wants used in his article, and I can click the "special instructions" button to see exactly what he expects from me. It is essential that I do this before I hit that "Write Article" button. When I click on "Special Instructions" this is what I see:

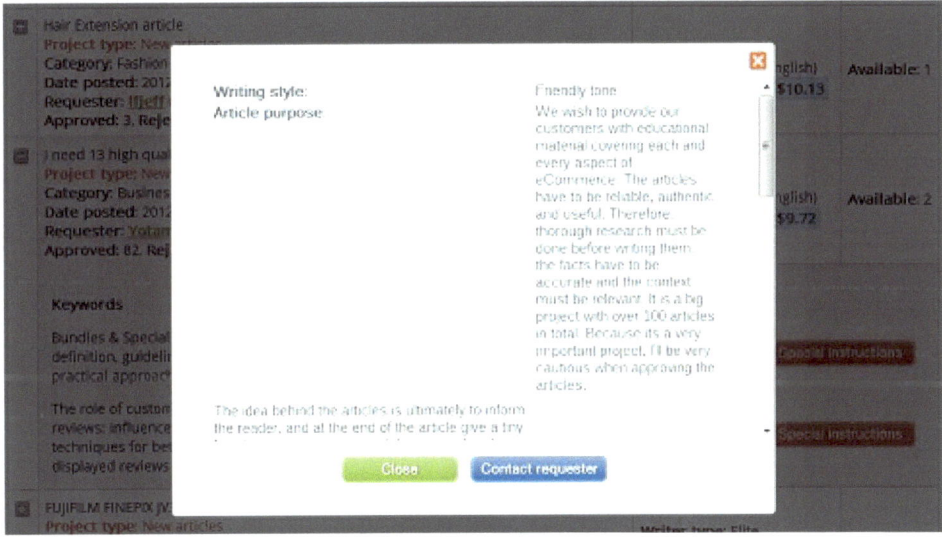

Here, I can see what any special requests or instructions that the requester has, and I can determine whether or not I want to write this article. I also have the option of contacting the requester to ask questions, but I rarely do this. If the instructions are not clear enough, I simply move on to another listing.

When I close this box, and click on "Write Article" this is what I see next:

This is the upper portion of the screen where I will work. It has a timer that is counting down. I have approximately three hours to complete this assignment. I also see how much I am being paid, the keywords that the requester wants used, and the project instructions. On the bottom portion of the page I see:

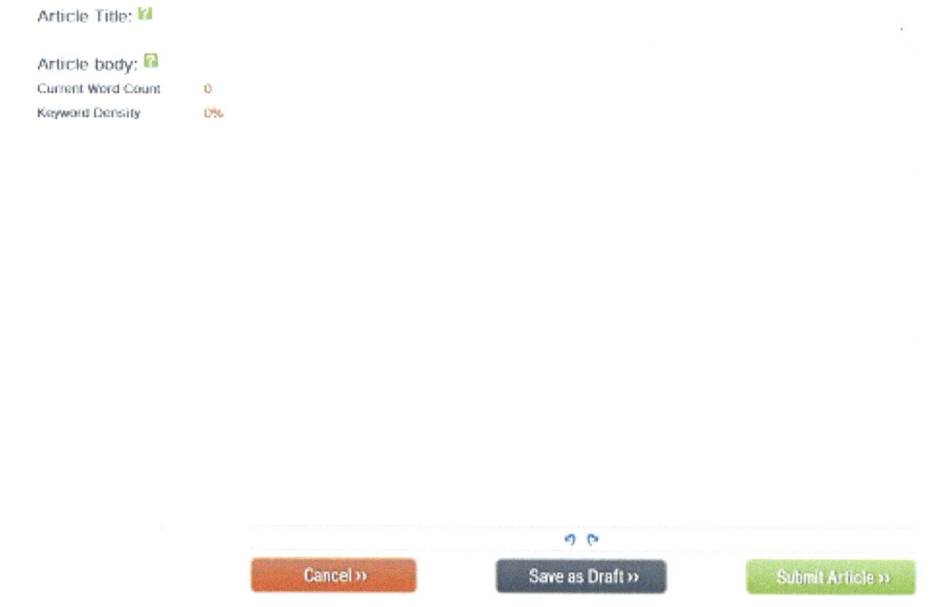

This is where I write the title for the article, and the article. On the left side of the page, you can see that there is a word count and a keyword density count. There is not, however, any spell checking or grammar checking available, which is why you copy and paste the work into your own word processor before you hit that "Submit Article" button at the bottom of the page.

If you decide to back out of the project, all you have to do is hit the "Cancel" button. You are not penalized for doing this, and the job goes back into the project list for other writers.

Once you have written your article, double check the instructions that the requester submitted once again to make sure that you have followed his guidelines. Check your word count and keyword density, and grammar and spelling. When you are satisfied that the spelling and grammar are perfect, that you have the proper word count, and the proper keyword density, click the "Submit Article" button.

**Important Note:** If keyword density matters, the requester will state this in his special instructions. If there is nothing about keyword density in those instructions, you can assume that it does not matter to this requester.

Once you have submitted the article, it is automatically run through CopyScape to check for originality. If you fail the CopyScape check too often, you will be banned from the site. Make sure that you are not copying and pasting other people's work and trying to pass it off as your own!

Now, at this point, assuming that you've passed the CopyScape check, the requester has 72 hours to approve your work. If he fails to do approve or reject the article in that time frame, the article is automatically approved, and the amount owed to you is added to your balance. Whether it is auto approved or manually approved, you get to rate the requester.

**This is important.** When you see that you have an article that needs your attention (which is displayed under the link for your inbox), the first thing that you want to do is go see the rating that the requester left for you. You can do this by clicking on the stars for your ratings on the upper left side of the screen.

If he left you a good rating, click the link under the inbox link, and leave him a good rating as well. If he left you a bad rating that you feel was undeserved, you are free to leave him a bad rating as well. With that said, just leave a star rating. Do not type in any comments at all. Being rude to a requester can get you banned, regardless of the reason.

If your article was rejected, you will not be paid for it. You still own the copyright to it. View the article, copy it, and go post it on your blog. This doesn't keep the requester from stealing it, but it doesn't do him much good to steal it and use it as is because Google will know that you published it first. His website will be penalized. You can check to see if your article has been stolen by using

CopyScape.com for free. If you do find that a requester stole your article, be sure to report him to iWriter.

Do not let a rejection deter you from your ultimate success. I've been writing for a long, long time, and I have rejected articles under my belt. Some of the requesters found through this site simply are not professional, and some are downright thieves. The majority, however, are good people to work with, and if they like your work, they are able to send you tips through the website, which adds to your weekly income.

Remember that this is the site that will pay you every week for the work that has been approved. Make sure that you are using this site each day. Set an income goal for your self, and you will easily be able to see how many articles you need to do each day through the site in order to reach that goal. This is the fastest possible way to make money when you first start out as a freelance writer.

If you have any questions about using iWriter.com, you can always contact their support by clicking the Contact button at the top of the page. You can also contact me through my site at www.contentwriterslife.com, and I will be happy to help you as much as I can.

### vWorker
### www.vworker.com

Once you have finished your work at iWriter, you will want to move over to vWorker. This is a bidding freelance site, with even more competition. At iWriter, you are able to get the work if you can click the button faster than other people. At vWorker, it isn't that easy at all.

You can opt to work strictly through iWriter if you want to, but I like having multiple sources of income. It just makes me feel more secure. An added bonus is that you can actually earn more money for the work through the bidding sites - if you are bidding on the right jobs, for the right amount of money, but you also have the added benefit of possibly landing a long term client or two.

In fact, every long term client that I've ever had came to me in one of two ways. Either they were a buyer that I had already worked for through vWorker, or a buyer that I worked for through vWorker referred me to someone that they knew who needed my writing services.

Private clients pay the best in this field, so you are probably wondering why I no longer write for private clients. Simply put, it is because of my health issue (Lupus). I need more leeway with my time, and working through these five sites alone affords me that leeway. I felt like it wasn't fair to my clients if I was constantly having to take time off or constantly having to push back deadlines, and I am happy with what I'm doing now anyway.

But if you do not have health problems that would cause you to be a hindrance to private clients, you should definitely work through the bidding freelance websites to land those clients, providing that you want private clients. Remember that private clients tend to control your time, whereas these sites, for the most part, really leave you in control of your time.

When you set up your profile on this site, you really need to be in a frame of mind to sell yourself. Buyers won't just look at how much you are bidding for their job, they will also be looking at your profile, and at any message that you send them with your bid.

When you sign up with vWorker, you will be led through the registration process. You will be asked to submit information for your W-9, and you will need to set up your pay options. When you get to the page for Alerts and Privacy, make sure that you look to the right and click the link to set your opt-in email settings. This way, you can get daily emails for newly listed projects, and you can choose which types of projects will and will not be included in that list. This makes it much easier to find the writing jobs.

Additionally, check the box for Match Maker Invitations. Many buyers use the Match Maker system to send bid notifications by email to those workers who match their needs. Getting notified quickly of new listings tends to make it easier to win jobs.

Trying to explain every aspect of vWorker would fill an entire encyclopedia collection, so I won't attempt that. What I will say is that you should take your time during the sign up process, and if you do not understand something, click the little question mark next to the item for an explanation.

Once you have finished the sign up process, click the link at the top of the page that says My Account, and then click My Dashboard from the drop down menu. This is where you can start looking for open job listings. Here is what the dashboard looks like:

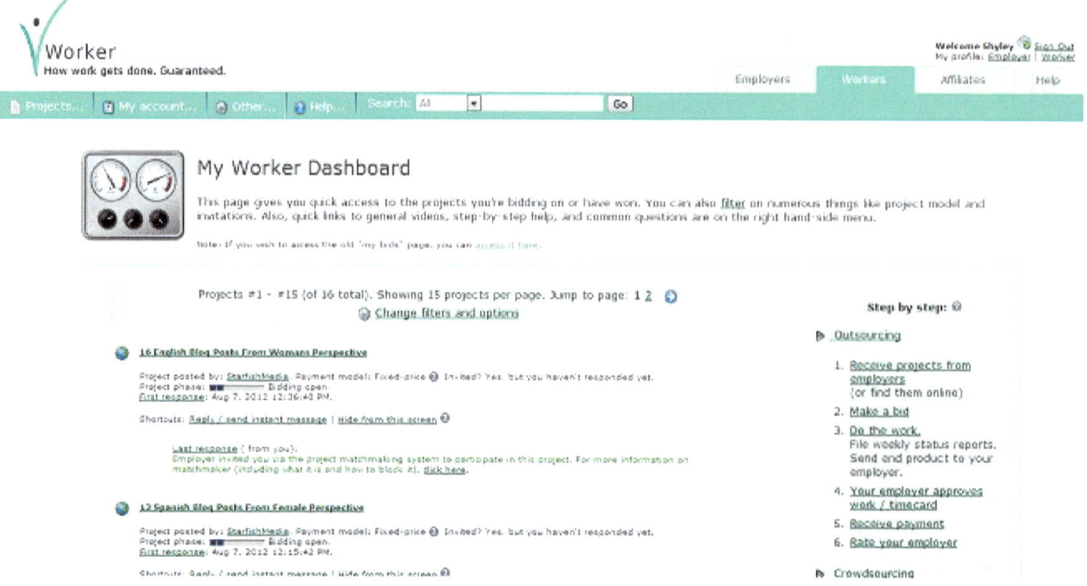

If I wanted to get more information about that first job listing on the page, I would simply click the headline, and then I will be taken to a page that gives me explicit details about the job.

The important things that you should look at on that next page include:

- The employers rating
- The deadline for the project
- The maximum bid accepted
- The detailed requirements (found toward the bottom of the page)

The questions you want to answer before bidding are:

1. Is the employer well rated? If not, do not work for that employer. Don't even bid on the job.

2. Can I meet the deadline for the job? If you can't, or if there is any doubt, do not bid on the job.

3. Is the maximum bid accepted a fair price for the work? If you do not feel that it is, do not bid on the job.

4. In the detailed requirements, is what the employer asks for within reason? If it isn't, or if it is confusing, do not bid on the job. However, if you want to, you can give the employer the opportunity to explain what he wants in greater detail by sending a message before you bid.

If you want to bid on the job, or contact the employer, click the link near the bottom of the page to do so.

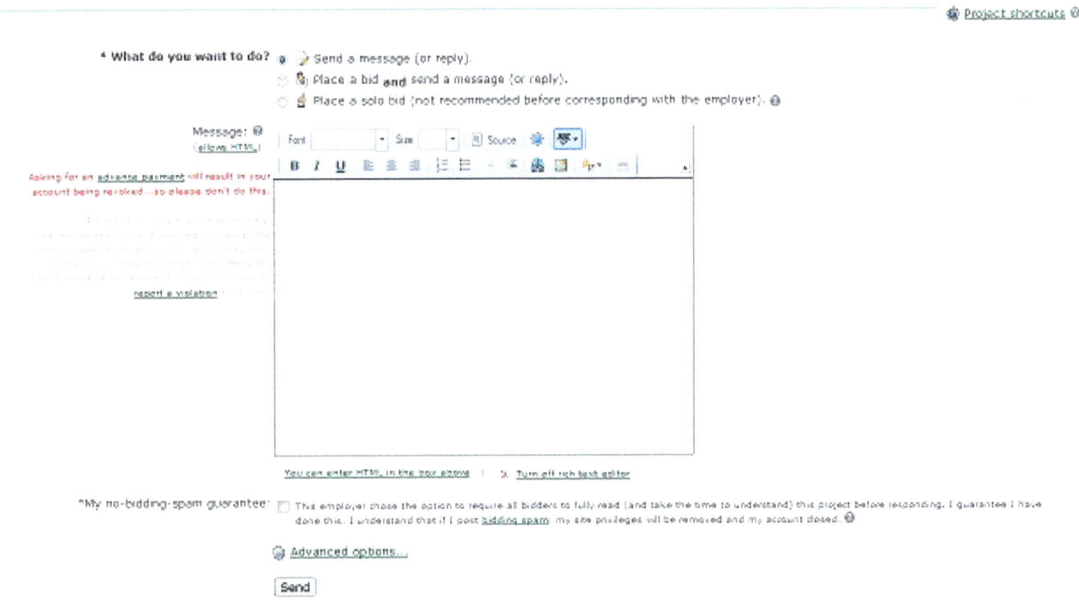

Here, you can send a message without a bid, place a bid and send a message, or just place a bid without a message. I recommend that you always place a bid with a message. When you click that option, the page expands just a bit and gives you a place to enter your bid amount, and also shows you once again what the maximum bid accepted is.

What I usually write in the message box varies, but I essentially let the employer know that if I am awarded the job, all work will be completed on time and as requested, and I thank him or her in advance for their consideration. You do not need to go on and on about your qualifications for the job. They will be looking at your profile, where that information should easily be found if you set up your profile right.

How much you bid is up to you, as long as you do not go over the maximum bid amount accepted by the employer. However, since you are new to the site, and you have no history or ratings on your profile, it is in your best interest to bid low. Bid low, win the bid, do an outstanding job, and you will have a great rating and at least one job in your job history. I recommend that you follow this formula for your first five or ten jobs at vWorker, and this will then allow you to command higher rates.

When a buyer, also known as an employer, accepts your bid, the funds to pay you are put into escrow. vWorker handles all of this for you, and you are notified via email that the funds have been escrowed, and that it is now okay to start work on the project. Those funds are held in escrow until one of several things happens:

1. You complete the job, submit the work, and the employer approves the work. At that time, the funds are released into your account at vWorker, to be paid out

to your PayPal account on the next payday. You get to set your own threshhold payment at vWorker. I advise that you set it to $0 so that you get paid each payday that there is money owed to you.

2. The job is cancelled. You have twenty four hours after the bid is accepted to cancel the job, without being penalized. In this case, the funds are released back to the buyer, not to you.

Along with the escrow system, which ensures that you get paid for the work that you do according to the buyer's instructions, vWorker also has an arbitration process in case you and the buyer do not agree on whether or not you've completed the work satisfactorily.

For freelance writers, the only way your work will be put into arbitration is if the work does not pass CopyScape, if the writing was horrible, or if you did not follow the buyer's requests in terms of keyword usage and things of this nature. However, if the issue is just spelling, punctuation, grammar, keyword usage or something of this nature, most buyers will simply ask you to rewrite the piece or make corrections.

Arbitration will occur, however, if you copied and pasted (plagiarized) work. Do not do this. Not only will you not get paid, you will not win the arbitration, and vWorker will give you a rating of 1 (horrible). If that ever happens, you may as well close out your account, because you are done at vWorker.

You also have the right to open an arbitration request. You should only do this if the buyer is asking for things beyond what the original request was, or if he or she is refusing to approve your work, or not answering your messages after a reasonable period of time. If you win the arbitration, the funds are released to you.

Some buyers at vWorker are tricky. One thing to be aware of is whether or not status reports are required for the project. If they are, you must log into the site, and submit your status reports each week, on time, as directed for each project that requires a status report. You can do a perfect job, and miss one status report, and not get paid.

When you submit your work, you will log into your account, and click on the link for your project, and then look on the right hand side of the page and click the link that says 'project shortcuts.'

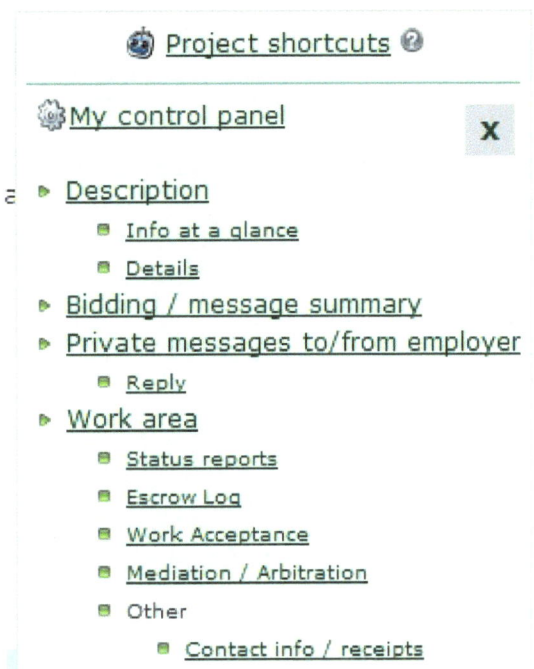

From there, click on Work Area, or Work Acceptance. As you can see, this is also where you would find status reports and where you would open or respond to arbitration. You would scroll down on the work area page to find the button to click to upload your file and report the work as complete.

**Important Note:** All files that you upload to vWorker must be zipped (compressed). If you have multiple articles for one buyer, you would put them all into one folder, right click on the folder, select 'send to,' and then select 'compressed (zipped) file.' This compressed file is the one that you will upload to the website.

Like iWriter, vWorker has a rating system. Once your work has been reported as complete by you, and accepted by the buyer, you can rate each other. Unlike iWriter, however, vWorker uses a blind rating system. You cannot see how you have been rated until after you and the buyer have rated each other. Should one of you not rate the other, the rating will not be visible for two weeks. This prevents retaliatory rating. After the two week period, if one of you has not rated the other, the option to submit a rating is closed.

As I mentioned before, you must be very careful not to submit too many bids at once through vWorker, and this is especially true when you are bidding low. You very well could win them all and find yourself unable to meet all of the deadlines. To start out, just bid on one or two jobs at a time at most, and once you win a bid, don't bid on another job until you are almost finished with the current job.

## *Write and Sell Your Content on Consignment*

When you write for iWriter or vWorker, you are limited to writing on topics that the buyer requests. When you write on consignment, however, you can write about any topic that you choose. You can also set your own prices.

Writing on consignment is just what it sounds like. For example, if you had a wedding dress that you wanted to sell, you might take it to a consignment shop. The shop owner will display your dress, and when someone purchases it, you get a cut of the purchase price, and the consignment shop gets a cut of the purchase price.

Content consignment works the same way. You write the article, submit it to the site, an editor either approves it or rejects it, and if it is approved, it is listed for sale. You don't have to worry about anything but writing great articles. You do not need to advertise anything because the consignment site does that for you, but you can promote your articles through other channels if you choose to do so, as long as the article is only being sold through the one consignment site.

The key to being successful through content consignment sites is in knowing what buyers are looking for. Typically, they want 'evergreen' content. What this means is that the content isn't dated in any way. The information in your article will be just as valuable and relevant tomorrow or next year as it is today.

You will also have more success if you write articles in the most profitable niches: wealth, relationships, and health. If your content provides information to help someone become wealthier, healthier, or happier, it will almost always sell if you have priced it right and it is well written.

There are actually very few sites where you can sell your content on consignment. I currently only work through one such site, Constant-Content. The reason why I currently only work through this site is because the going rates for articles is decent.

Even though you can set your own prices, you do not want to cut your own throat by setting your price too far above what everyone else is charging for comparable articles in terms of quality, topic, and length. Also, among the few content consignment sites that exist, Constant-Content seems to get the most traffic from buyers.

Signing up for an account at Constant-Content is very easy and fast. There are no hoops to jump through. You can use a pen name on the site, and of course, you also need to include your real information so that you can get paid, including your PayPal email address.

After you sign up, you will want to set up your profile and include a short bio that pertains to your writing skills. You cannot use website links in your profile, but you can refer to your profiles on other writing sites if you like, as long as you do not link to them.

There are four options for writing articles at Constant-Content, as follows:

**1. Write on Consignment -** Choose a topic of your choice, and write your article in Microsoft Word or Open Office, and submit it to the site.

**2. Public Requests -** Buyers can submit public requests for articles. You can read the details of the request, write the article, and submit it. If your article is chosen, the buyer purchases it. If it is not chosen, it becomes a consignment article, and is up for sale with your other articles. Public Requests can be seen by all writers on the site, and all writers are free to submit an article for each request.

**3. Private Requests -** Often, if a buyer has purchased articles written by you in the past, he or she will offer you private requests. You have the option to accept the assignment or to turn it down. No other writers will see this request - it is yours if you want it.

**4. Writer's Pool -** You will not see the tab for the Writer's Pool until you have ten articles that have been approved by the editors, and you have a record of submitting error free work. When you see the Writer's Pool Settings on the left side of the screen you will know that you can apply for the various writer's pools that are available, if you choose to do so.

You must apply for the different types of writing assignments that are offered through the writer's pool...if you do not apply, and submit a writing sample for that type of writing, no writer's pool assignments will be offered to you. Again, you cannot even apply until the Writer's Pool Settings option appears on the My Account box, as seen here:

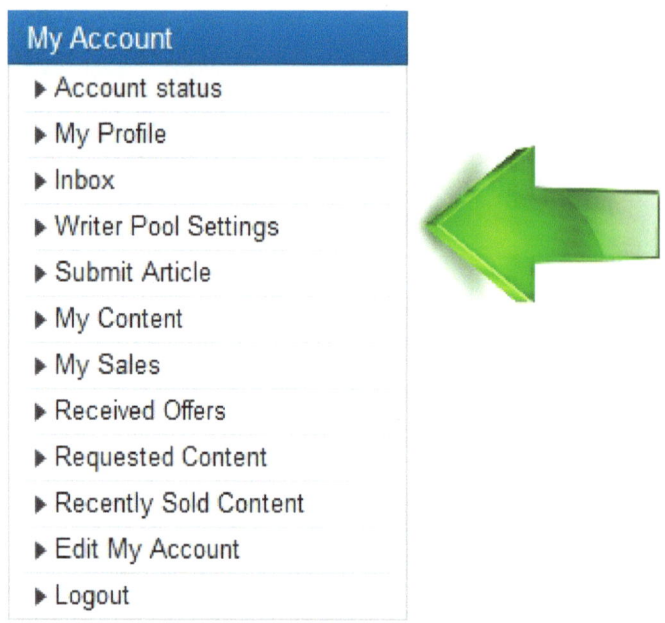

Regardless of which option you choose for writing, all articles that you write will go through the editors before it is available for sale, even if the article is for a request. Of the few existing content consignment sites out there, Constant-Content editors are believed to be the absolute toughest. I once had an article rejected because I used a comma where the editor didn't think I needed one. I didn't complain - I just simply removed the comma, resubmitted the work, and it was accepted.

It takes anywhere from two to five days for your article to be accepted or rejected. If the article is rejected, read the editors comments very carefully to see what they want changed. Make the necessary changes, and resubmit it following the instructions on the website. If you have made the changes that were requested, it is almost guaranteed approval.

If writing for requests makes you happy, do so. I personally choose to write mostly on consignment because I have more freedom with the topics that I choose. You can use all available methods for submitting content to the site - requests, consignment, writer's pool and private requests...it doesn't matter, as long as you are submitting something to the site everyday.

Submitting content to the site every day is not a requirement of the site. It is a requirement for success. The more content you have in your 'inventory' the more money you will earn through the site. The site has a 70% to 80% sales rate. This means that out of every 100 articles you write, you will sell between seventy and eighty of them.

If you are pricing all of your articles at $30 for full rights, and you sell 70 of them that amounts to $2100. Unfortunately, you do not get the full $2100. Constant-

Content has to get paid too, and they currently take 35% of each of your sales. Therefore, your cut would actually be $1365. That 35% is something that you have to take into account when you price your articles. So, if you truly want $30 for your article, you need to price it at about $46.

Many writer's feel that 35% is too much of a cut for Constant-Content, but if you think about it, that's not really true. You have to think about the services that are offered to you as a writer with your account. First, it costs nothing to sign up at Constant-Content. You do not have to advertise. You do not have to bid on jobs. They edit your work to ensure that the work that buyers are seeing is absolutely perfect. They collect the payments from the buyers. They maintain this awesome platform at no additional charge to you. They make sure that you get paid each month, directly to your PayPal account. The list of what they are offering you goes on and on, so for me, personally, I think 35% is reasonable.

When you submit an article, you will choose which rights, or licenses, are available with your article. The choices are usage, unique, and full rights. Let's take a look at each license.

**Usage:** The buyer can use the article as it is. He or she cannot change the article or add to it. Your name stays intact as the author. The article remains for sale, but only with usage rights available. The article can be resold over and over again for usage rights only.

**Unique:** The buyer can use the article as it is. He or she cannot change the article or add to it. Your name stays intact as the author. The article is removed from the articles for sale - nobody else can purchase it.

**Full Rights:** The buyer can do whatever they like with the article, and remove your name as the author. They can even replace your name with their own as the author. Nobody else can purchase it, as it is removed from the articles for sale.

When you submit your article, you must make it available for usage rights, and currently you cannot set that price below $7. You can choose to also make it available for Unique and Full Rights, or just Unique Rights, or just Full Rights. Constant-Content has a suggested price chart that you can elect to use, or not use.

**co constantcontent**

This document is to help writers price their work. This document is only to give writers an **idea** on how to price the articles/content they submit. Every subject is different, some subjects will pay lower and others will pay higher. Of course prices can vary based on the writer's skill, background and experience.

If you're unsure about what each license is and means please read up on the differences between Usage, Unique and Full Rights licenses

| Number of Words | Usage Price | Unique Price | Full Rights Price |
|---|---|---|---|
| 300-600 | $10-$25 | $30-$60 | $40-$80 |
| 600-800 | $25-$35 | $60-$80 | $80-$100 |
| 800-1000 | $35-$45 | $80-$100 | $100-$120 |
| 1000-1200 | $45-$55 | $100-$120 | $120-$150 |
| 1200-1500 | $55-$65 | $120-$150 | $150-$180 |
| 1500-2000 | $65-$75 | $150-$200 | $180-$250 |

Note that these are just suggested prices. You are free to set your own prices, as long as they are not set below $7.

Now, different writers on Constant-Content use different strategies for pricing articles. Some will set all three prices the same. For example, the writer will set the usage rights at $30, the unique rights at $30, and the full rights at $30. The theory is that most buyers want unique rights at the very least, and often only want full rights.

They want to be the only one publishing the work. If they see that someone has already purchased usage rights, they will pass it by. Even if they only wanted usage rights, if all of the pricing is the same, they may as well go ahead and buy the full rights if they want the article. This strategy works very well for many people.

Another strategy that is often used is to only list the article with usage rights, and not offer unique or full rights. Once the article has been sold for usage rights, you can use the article as well on other sites, such as your own blog or other paid publishing platforms that allow previously published content. In the past, I've set different prices for each license, and I've sold each license type, but I'm seriously considering using the 'price all licenses the same' strategy to see how that works out.

As mentioned before, if you write on topics that pertain to health, wealth, or relationships (happiness), you work will most likely sell. It may not sell immediately, but it will eventually sell - as long as the content is evergreen. With that said, however, there are a couple of tools that you can make excellent use of at Constant-Content.

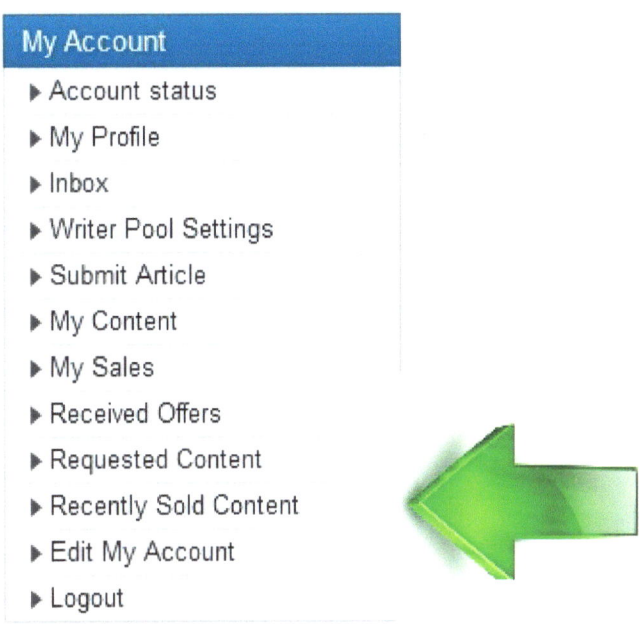

If you click on Recently Sold Content, you can see which articles have sold through Constant-Content recently. These are not just your recently sold articles - this is all recently sold content. This tells you what buyers are looking for.

| Document | Type | Price | Category | Date |
|---|---|---|---|---|
| 6 Loaded Interview Questions and How You Should Answer | fullrights | $22.00 | > Business > Careers | 08/08/2012 |
| Acer Threatens to Dump Microsoft Software From Its PCs | fullrights | $27.00 | > Technology > Computers | 08/08/2012 |
| Are Hybrid Fruits and Vegetables Healthy - or Not? | fullrights | $55.00 | > Health & Lifestyles > Nutrition | 08/08/2012 |
| What Should You Bring on a Timeshare Stay? | fullrights | $50.00 | > Recreation > Travel | 08/08/2012 |
| Understanding the Co-Insurance Penalty | fullrights | $34.00 | > Private Request | 08/08/2012 |
| Alterna BAMBOO Shine Express Shopper | fullrights | $50.00 | > Private Request | 08/08/2012 |
| Alterna BAMBOO UV Color Protection Express Shopper | fullrights | $50.00 | > Private Request | 08/08/2012 |
| Alterna Hair Sprays Express Shopper Page | fullrights | $50.00 | > Private Request | 08/08/2012 |
| CosMedix Brand Page | fullrights | $50.00 | > Private Request | 08/08/2012 |
| Philosophy Brand Page Top Content | fullrights | $30.00 | > Private Request | 08/08/2012 |

Not only that, but you can also see what has been sold in specific categories, and what search terms buyers have used to search for articles by using the tabs at the top: Articles, Categories, and Search Topics. This is a very, very useful tool when you are wondering what you will write about today!

Again, when you write for Constant-Content, you will write in your own word processing software. When you are ready to submit an article, click on the link in your account box that says Submit Article. You will see this:

| | |
|---|---|
| Title * (Auto-Capitalize ☑ ) | Please make sure that your title is capitalized properly |
| Category * | -- Select Category -- ▾ |
| File * (.txt, .doc or .rtf only) | Choose File No file chosen<br>Must be either a .txt, .doc or .rtf file |
| Is This For A Requests? | -- Not For A Request -- ▾ |
| Word Count * | |
| Usage Price * | $ ____ USD (Must be greater than $7.00 Why?) |
| Unique Price ☑ | $ ____ USD |
| Full Rights Price ☑ | $ ____ USD |
| Short Summary *<br>This is the first experience publishers have with your work. It needs to be unique NOT an excerpt from the article. It should be at least three sentences long | |
| Content Excerpt *<br>Please make sure that your excerpt contains<br>At least 1/3 of your article<br>Breaks between paragraphs<br>Single spaced lines<br>No strange formatting such as errant capitals, or unexpected line breaks | |
| Keywords (comma separated)<br>Keywords are used in the search mechanism so including relevant keywords will help customers to find your article. | |
| Best Offer | ☐ Check this to allow customers to make offers on this article |
| Discount Offer | ☐ Check this to allow this article to be included in discount packages |
| | Submit Article |

Here, you paste in the title of your article, and leave the Auto Capitalize box checked. Select the category for your article, and attach the file. If you have written this for a request, you choose the proper request from the drop down box. If it is not for a request, you leave that set at 'not for a request.'

For the word count, use the word count feature in your word processing software to get the count, but do not include the number of words in the article title - just the body of the article. Set your prices, as discussed earlier. In the short summary, you must essentially describe what your article is about. This is your opportunity to sell the article to those who may be interested. You cannot use any text from the article, however, in this section. Use two or three sentences, and keep the whole thing under fifty words.

Open up your calculator and divide the word count for the article by three. If your article is 500 words long, you would copy and paste the first 167 words of your article into the Content Excerpt box. This and the summary are the only things that the potential buyer will be able to see of your article without making a purchase.

In the bottom section, list keywords that pertain to your article, separated by commas. The bottom two things on the submission form make it possible for buyers to make you offers on the article, and allow Constant-Content to make your article part of package deals. I do not check these boxes, but this is entirely up to you. I cannot comment further on these two boxes since I've not had any experience with them.

Once you've got everything filled out, double check it and then triple check it. Make sure you've attached the article, and then hit the submit button. Now, you just have to wait for it to be approved or rejected.

While you are waiting, you can browse through the help files on the site, or visit the writer's forum and join the community. You could also go write more articles at iWriter or move onto the next phase of freelance writing - paid publishing platforms.

**Important Tip:** Use the widget that is available from Constant-Content to add a feed on your blog of the articles that you have for sale at Constant Content.

## *Working through Paid Publishing Platforms*

Many of the Paid Publishing Platform sites today operate much like Constant-Content; with one exception...you rarely sell an article for upfront pay. Instead, your content is published on the site, and you get paid a share of the revenue from advertising based on page views of your article.

The paid publishing platform site that I use is Yahoo! Contributor Network. I've only recently signed up with Helium, which is reported to be another excellent site of this type, but as a newcomer to this site, I won't include information regarding it in this book because I've not learned enough about it to do so.

As with Constant-Content, the more articles you submit, the more money you will make. This income however is so varied and so unpredictable that you should not count it when you are writing to earn money to pay your bills. Count any income you earn through this type of site as bonus money, with no set dollar amount.

You are probably wondering why you should even bother with this type of platform if the pay is so sporadic and varied. I do this for the long term benefits. I consider each article that I submit as future residual income or passive income if you will. I write the article once, and as long as it is evergreen, it can continue to bring in drops of income here and there for a very long time - possibly forever, regardless of the amount of income that it is. That is why it is important to submit lots of articles. I suggest that you submit one article per day to at least one paid publishing platform.

This is an excellent platform for freelance writers, and for me personally, it is very refreshing to write about topics that are of interest to me after writing my daily quota of articles on topics that are of interest to someone else. This is where you can really spread your wings as a freelance writer.

**Just a tip:** When you publish content on any paid publishing platform site, you will want to link to it on your blog. Ideally, you should do this in a post on your blog, but make sure that you do not post the exact same article...just refer to it and link to it. Then you can share your blog post on all of your social networking sites, such as Twitter and Facebook. This drives traffic to your blog post, and ultimately to your content on the paid publishing site, which of course increases your income from that site.

*Yahoo! Contributor Network*
*contributor.yahoo.com*

Signing up for a Yahoo! Contributor Network account isn't hard, but it is a long process. Allow yourself a couple of hours to complete the signup process, and follow the directions carefully. Sign up with your real name and information. If you want to use a pen name, this can be set up in your account after you are all signed up and verified.

Once you are signed up, do not start submitting content right away. Take the time to read everything. Start by clicking the Help link at the top of your page after you log into your account. Yahoo offers great advice to writers. Take that advice if you want to be successful.

Also, take the time to do all of the courses in the Yahoo Contributor Network Academy. This is the best free web content writing education you ever will get, and completing all of the courses will make you eligible for more assignments on the assignment desk, if you are interested in assignments.

When you submit content to Yahoo, it is not immediately published. Human editors look over it first. After it is approved, it will be published - or you may be offered an upfront payment for it. If an upfront payment is offered, the article may or may not still be eligible for performance payments as well. You will be told this when the upfront payment offer is made.

Yahoo pays via PayPal once a month for performance payments. You must be 18 years old, and you must be a United States Citizen or legal resident of the United States. If you are not a citizen or legal resident of the United States, you may still be able to earn money through the Yahoo Featured Contributor program. Upfront payments are paid within a day or two of you accepting the offer.

You must keep your Yahoo Contributor Network account active by logging in at least once every 90 days. If you do not log in once every 90 days, your account will be closed, and any performance payments that have been earned, but not yet paid out will be forfeited.

Submitting content to the site is fairly easy and very similar to submitting content to Constant-Content. There is one exception, however, and it confuses many people. You must choose whether the content you are submitting is being submitted with Exclusive Rights, Non-Exclusive Rights, or Display Only Rights.

**Exclusive Rights:** This is the box you should check if your content is original and you will not be submitting it or publishing it elsewhere - and it has not already been submitted or published elsewhere. When the article is accepted, it belongs to Yahoo or one of their partner sites. The content does, however, retain your name as the author. This type of license makes the content eligible for both up front payments and performance payments.

**Non-Exclusive Rights:** This is the box to check if the content is original, but you still want the right to publish the content elsewhere later on. It is still eligible for up front payments, but the payment offer is less likely, and even if an offer is made, it is greatly reduced. The work is still eligible for performance payments.

**Display Only Rights:** This is the option to choose for content that you have published elsewhere. It will not be eligible for up front payments, but it is still eligible for performance payments. Remember those articles that sold for usage rights at Constant-Content? These fit nicely into this category.

Another difference between submitting articles to Yahoo and submitting to Constant-Content is that you will be typing your article into a text box on site with Yahoo Contributor Network. Additionally, you can add photos that are relevant to your article and supporting links.

Yahoos does an excellent job of leading you through each step of the submission process, and until you've fully gotten the hang of it, make sure that you read everything available to you when you are submitting articles.

As you might imagine, there are thousands of submissions made each day to Yahoo Contributor Network. Each submission is proofread by a human being, so the approval process is slow. It can take up to two weeks for approval or rejection.

Before I wrap up this section on Paid Publishing Platforms, I want to stress again the importance of reading everything that Yahoo offers you concerning being a contributor. I also want to again stress the value and importance of taking the time to make good use of the courses offered for free through the Yahoo! Contributor Network Academy, which is accessible through your dashboard when you log into the site. If you truly want to be a success on this site, take the time to do these things before you submit anything at all, no matter how long it takes.

## *Part 3: Action Steps to Take*

You now have all of the information that you need to start earning a living as a freelance writer. It is up to you to take action and make the plan work for you. Here is a check list of everything that you need to do, just so that it is all clear for you:

☐ Get a computer if you do not already have one.

☐ Get internet access.

☐ Obtain Word Processing Software (Microsoft Word or Open Office).

☐ Open either a Premium or Business PayPal Account at www.paypal.com.

☐ Take the writing test at www.edufind.com/english/grammar/.

☐ If needed, take the free writing course at esl.about.com/c/ec/20.htm.

☐ Get familiar with Grammarly at www.grammarly.com.

☐ Study the format of articles at www.ezinearticles.com.

☐ Set up a system to keep track of website addresses, usernames and passwords, income and expenses and article topics that sell well, as well as article ideas.

☐ Schedule your work time.

☐ Start your own blog at www.blogger.com or at www.wordpress.com.

☐ Sign up at www.iWriter.com. Read all of the information they provide.

☐ Set up your profile at iWriter.

☐ Write and submit articles at iWriter to achieve Elite Status.

☐ Determine how much money you need to earn each week, and divide that by the number of days that you will write each week. Write that number of articles for each day that you write at iWriter, since this is your 'steady' income.

☐ Link to your iWriter profile on your blog.

☐ Sign up at www.vWorker.com. Read all of the information that they provide.

☐ Set up your profile at vWorker.

☐ Search for and bid on one or two jobs at vWorker. Do the articles as you win the bids.

☐ Link to your vWorker profile on your blog.

☐ Sign up at www.Constant-Content.com. Read all of the information they have.

☐ Set up your profile at Constant-Content.com.

☐ Write and submit at least one article per day at Constant-Content.com

☐ Get the widget from Constant-Content.com for your blog.

☐ Sign up at Yahoo! Contributor Network at contributor.yahoo.com. Read everything that they offer.

☐ Take the courses through the Yahoo! Contributor Network Academy.

☐ Set up your profile at Yahoo! Contributor Network.

☐Write and submit at least one article per day to Yahoo! Contributor Network.

☐Link to your Yahoo! Contributor Network profile on your blog.

☐Link to published content on Yahoo! Contributor Network in your blog posts.

☐Check out the additional resources in Part 4 of this book to find even more places that will pay you for your writing skills.

☐Get Paid!

# Part 4: Additional Resources

Here, you will find additional sites that will pay you for your writing skills. I have little or no experience with these sites, so I cannot tell you much about them. If you want additional sources of income other than the ones covered in detail, these are sites that you can check out for potential opportunities. This list is does not cover all of the sites that offer writing opportunities. These are just the most well known sites.

## Other Freelance Websites: Bid and No Bid Platforms

### Bid Platforms

ODesk
www.odesk.com

iFreelance
www.ifreelance.com

elance
www.elance.com

Guru
www.guru.com

Freelancer
www.freelancer.com

ozLance
www.ozlance.com

### No Bid Platforms

Pure Content
www.purecontent.com

TextBroker
www.textbroker.com

London Brokers
www.londonbrokers.net

Writer Access
www.writeraccess.com

Skyword
www.skyword.com

Interact Media
www.interactmedia.com

Article Document
www.articledocument.com

WiseGeek
www.wisegeek.com

## *Other Content Consignment Sites*

GhostBlogger
www.ghostblogger.net

Demand Studios
www.demandstudios.com

Article Sale
www.articlesale.com

## *Other Paid Publishing Platforms*

Populis
www.populis.com

Hub Pages
www.hubpages.com

Squidoo
www.squidoo.com

Helium
www.helium.com

Gather
www.gather.com

Triond
www.triond.com

Factoidz
factoidz.com